CULTURE IN ACTION

How to Read a Work of Art

Laura J. Hensley

Raintree

Chicago, Illinois

www.heinemannraintree.com
Visit our website to find out more information about Heinemann-Raintree books.

To order:
☎ Phone 888-454-2279
💻 Visit www.heinemannraintree.com to browse our catalog and order online.

©2011 Raintree
an imprint of Capstone Global Library, LLC
Chicago, Illinois

Edited by Louise Galpine, Megan Cotugno, and Abby Colich
Designed by Ryan Frieson
Original illustrations ©Capstone Global Library, Ltd.
Illustrated by Cavedweller Studio, Randy Schirz
Picture research by Liz Alexander
Originated by Capstone Global Library, Ltd.
Printed and bound in China by China Translation & Printing Services, Ltd.

14 13 12 11 10
10 9 8 7 6 5 4 3 2 1

Library of Congress Cataloging-in-Publication Data
Hensley, Laura.
  How to read a work of art / Laura Hensley. -- 1st ed.
    p. cm. -- (Culture in action)
  Includes bibliographical references and index.
  ISBN 978-1-4109-3925-8 (hc)
  1. Art--Juvenile literature. 2. Art appreciation--Juvenile literature. I. Title.
  N7440.H27 2011
  701'.1--dc22
                    2009051183

Acknowledgments

The author and publishers are grateful to the following for permission to reproduce copyright material:

We would like to thank the following for permission to reproduce photographs: Alamy pp. **11** (© Craig Lovell/Eagle Visions Photography), **27** (© Roger Bamber); The Art Archive pp. **6** (National Gallery London/Eileen Tweedy), **10** (Musée du Château de Versailles/Alfredo Dagli Orti), **14** (National Gallery London/ Eileen Tweedy), **20** (Gemaldegalerie Dresden), **22** (Musée du Louvre Paris/Gianni Dagli Orti); © 2010 Banco de México Diego Rivera Frida Kahlo Museums Trust, Mexico, D.F./DACS p. **16** (The Art Archive/Museum of Modern Art Mexico/Gianni Dagli Orti); © Carrie Mae Weems/Courtesy Artist and Jack Shainman Gallery, New York p. **23**; Corbis pp. **7** (© The Gallery Collection), **8** (© Historical Picture Archive), **15** (© Guenter Rossenbach), **19** (© Angelo Hornak), **21** (© Chris Rainier), **25** (© The Andy Warhol Foundation); © The Pollock-Krasner Foundation ARS, NY and DACS, London 2010 p. **26** (The Art Archive/Galleria d'Arte Moderna Milan/Alfredo Dagli Orti); © Sebastiao Salgado/ Amazonas/nbpictures p. **13**; © Succession Picasso/DACS, London 2010 p. **12** (The Art Archive/Reina Sofia Museum Madrid); The Royal Collection © 2009, Her Majesty Queen Elizabeth II p. **4**; Shutterstock p. **18** (© Amy Nichole Harris).

Cover photograph of *The Arnolfini Portrait* (1434) by Jan van Eyck reproduced with permission of The Art Archive (National Gallery London/Eileen Tweedy).

We would like to thank Susie Hodge and Jackie Murphy for their invaluable help in the preparation of this book.

Every effort has been made to contact copyright holders of any material reproduced in this book. Any omissions will be rectified in subsequent printings if notice is given to the publisher.

Author
Laura J. Hensley is an editor and writer who specializes in topics related to art and literature.

Literacy consultant
Jackie Murphy is Director of Arts at the Center of Teaching and Learning, Northeastern Illinois University. She works with teachers, artists, and school leaders internationally.

Expert
Susie Hodge is an author and artist with nearly 60 books in print. She has an MA in the History of Art from the University of London and is a Fellow of the Royal Society of Arts. She teaches and lectures on practical art and art and design history to students of all ages.

Contents

Some words are printed in bold, **like this**. You can find out what they mean by looking in the glossary on page 30.

Approaching Art

You probably see works of art all the time, whether in your school, at home, or in a museum. But how often do you look closely at art, rather than simply glancing at it?

If you look closely, you will find that works of art are full of fascinating stories and ideas. Reading, or **interpreting**, art means looking for this meaning. It means finding out what the artist was trying to communicate through a work of art.

To interpret a work of art, ask yourself some questions:

• Who or what is shown in the work?

• What is the **context** or background? Where was the work made? What was going on in history at the time?

• What are the symbols in the work?

• What do you know about the artist?

• What do you notice about the work's **formal elements**, such as line and color?

Think about artists and the world they lived in. Painter Artemisia Gentileschi made this self-portrait in Italy in the 1630s.

In the end, there is often no single "correct" interpretation of a work of art. Everyone sees and experiences things differently. But if you ask enough questions and think deeply about the work, your interpretation is as worthwhile as any expert's. That is the fun of interpreting art!

Use this map to see where the works of public art mentioned in this book were made.

1. California:
Carrie Mae Weems's *Family Pictures and Stories* (page 23)

2. Mexico City, Mexico:
Frida Kahlo's *The Two Fridas* (page 16)

3. Tikal, Guatemala:
ancient stela monument (page 11)

4. São Paolo, Brazil:
Sebastião Salgado's *Migrations* photograph series (page 13)

5. New York City:
Andy Warhol's *Campbell's Soup Cans* (page 25)
Jackson Pollock's *Painting A* (page 26)

6. Suffolk, England:
John Constable's *The Hay Wain* (page 6)

7. London, England:
Anish Kapoor's *C-Curve* (page 27)

8. Guernica, Spain:
Pablo Picasso's *Guernica* (page 12)

9. Paris, France
Jacques-Louis David's *Coronation of Napoleon* (page 10)

10. Giverny, France:
Claude Monet's *The Poppy Field near Giverny* (page 7)

11. Belgium:
Jan van Eyck's *The Arnolfini Portrait* (cover, page 14)

12. Rome, Italy:
Artemisia Gentileschi's self portrait (page 4)
statue of Marcus Aurelius (page 15)
Raphael's *Sistine Madonna* (page 20)

13. Netherlands:
Johannes Vermeer's *The Lacemaker* (page 22)

14. Zimbabwe:
Zimbabwe tribal mask (page 21)

15. Tamil Nadu, India:
statue of Shiva (page 19)

16. Hong Kong:
Tian Tan Buddha (*Big Buddha*) (page 18)

17. Japan:
Katsushika Hokusai's *The Great Wave at Kanagawa* (page 8)

The Natural World

Since prehistoric cave paintings, artists have captured the natural world. Artists create their own interpretations of the nature around them.

Details of nature

English artist John Constable's *The Hay Wain*, from 1821, shows a peaceful **landscape** (view of nature) in Suffolk, England. Workers move through a river. In the far right background are haymakers. In terms of its **formal elements**, Constable captures each detail with almost scientific exactness. The scene is well ordered and peaceful.

The title of Constable's *The Hay Wain* (1821) refers to a horse-drawn cart that carries hay.

The **context** is important. This landscape shows an actual place from Constable's happy childhood. But by the time Constable made the painting, the **Industrial Revolution** was causing factories and machines to spread across the countryside. Workers also wanted better treatment.

So, why did Constable make this exact record of a place? Maybe he wanted to record a world that was dear to him, before it changed forever.

Impressionism

In the 1870s, a group of French artists created a style called **Impressionism**. They wanted to capture quick "impressions" oftentimes of nature. To experience nature directly, they painted outdoors.

Claude Monet was a leading Impressionist. In works like *The Poppy Field near Giverny* (1885) the shapes and outlines are sketchy. The color is also unnatural. Monet used quick brushstrokes (marks made by a paintbrush) to create a bright, glistening quality. This effect copies how the eye sees nature in bright sunlight.

Monet's painting is not about the exact way things appear. Rather, it is about playing with things like brushstroke and color. It is also about the experience of being outdoors.

Many people were shocked that works like Monet's *The Poppy Field near Giverny* (1885) looked sketchy and unfinished.

Hokusai's *The Great Wave at Kanagawa* (1832) was part of a series of prints.

Japanese woodblock printing

Katsushika Hokusai was part of a long Japanese tradition of **woodblock printing** (see box). His print *The Great Wave at Kanagawa* (1832) shows a moment frozen in time.

A falling wave

Hokusai used beautiful, crisp lines to show the outlines of the wave. The wave is also the center of the **composition**. These formal elements bring the viewer's eye to the wave.

The viewer feels a disaster is about to happen—the giant wave will crash down on the small men in the boats. Also, the tips of the wave seem almost frightening, like hands reaching toward the men.

Color woodblock printing

To make a color woodblock print, an artist carves a series of different shapes into several wooden blocks. Each block is dipped in a different color of ink and pressed onto paper. Prints from all the different blocks and colors combine to make a final image.

Create your own nature scenes

Steps to follow:

1. Think of a landscape or nature scene that means a lot to you. If possible, visit the place yourself, but otherwise you can work from a photograph or from memory. You will paint this favorite place in three different ways.

2. Imagine you are a painter like Constable and want to show every detail. Try to capture every tree and building exactly as it appears before you.

3. Imagine you are an Impressionist. This time focus on creating a quick impression of the scene, like grass blowing.

4. Finally, imagine you are an artist like Hokusai. Try to capture a smaller, active detail within the scene, like ducks swimming.

5. Hang all three works for your friends and family to see.

Which of your three works do you think captures the scene the best? Why?

Focus on the parts of a landscape that you respond to the most.

Recording History

A key function of art since ancient times has been to record history. One such historical event is the **coronation** of the French emperor Napoleon.

Napoleon's coronation

Beginning in 1805, French artist Jacques-Louis David created a painting to record the coronation (crowning) of the French emperor Napoleon. The historical **context** is that Napoleon was taking power away from the Catholic Church. This made some people uneasy. Napoleon wanted this painting to convince people of his right to power.

The size of David's *Coronation of Napoleon* (1805–7)—20.3 by 32.1 feet (6.2 by 9.8 meters)—adds to its sense of importance.

A court artist

David was Napoleon's official artist. He could be trusted to create a painting supporting his employer. For example, in this work he showed Napoleon crowning his wife, Josephine. The Catholic pope had previously had this power to crown people. So, in his painting, David showed Napoleon's power over the church.

Focusing on Napoleon

David's use of **formal elements** also supports Napoleon's power. Napoleon is the source of action near the center of the **composition**, where the viewer's eye travels. The pope is off to the side. Also, the pope's chair is low so that Napoleon (who was in fact small) looks big by comparison.

Knowing these details, does Napoleon's coronation still seem as grand?

Monuments

Monuments (large works of public art) have been used since ancient times to record history. This **stela** (stone slab) is from Tikal, in present-day Guatemala, from the 400s CE. The carvings present the achievements of a leader. He would have ordered an artist to create this work and place it in front of a public temple.

The public location of this stela (400s CE) forced everyone to notice it.

11

Picasso's *Guernica* is huge, at 11.5 by 25.5 feet (3.5 by 7.8 meters). Its size adds to its power.

Guernica

Spanish artist Pablo Picasso made the painting *Guernica* in 1937 to represent another historical event. The context was that there was a war between the Spanish government and the forces of General Francisco Franco. On April 27, 1937, Franco's forces, helped by Germany, bombed the small town of Guernica, Spain. Hundreds of people were killed.

What does it show?

Picasso's painting shows a series of images: a woman with a dead child, an injured horse crushing a soldier, a bull, suffering people, and cut-off limbs. Some people have **interpreted** that the bull is supposed to be a symbol of the artist himself. Some think the horse represents Franco. No matter what the symbols mean, the horror and suffering in the scene are clear.

Lessons of Cubism

Picasso became famous in the early 1900s for the style called **Cubism**. *Guernica's* broken-apart shapes and flat space reflect the Cubist style. The broken-apart shapes also show the destruction caused by war. Some say this is the most powerful work of antiwar art in history.

Compare this to David's *Coronation* on page 10. Which style do you think records history the best? Why?

Sebastião Salgado and photojournalism

Photojournalists take photographs that capture real historical events as they happen. Brazilian photojournalist Sebastião Salgado captures historic trends like **migration**, the movement of large numbers of people. Salgado says he wants to make people think about other people and their suffering. Do you think this photograph achieves this goal?

This photo from Salgado's *Migrations* series shows Rwandans in a refugee camp.

Portraits

Artists have made portraits of other people—and of themselves—throughout history. These portraits let us know what people looked like long ago.

A famous portrait

Jan van Eyck, an artist who worked in Bruges (in present-day Belgium), created *The Arnolfini Portrait* in 1434. It shows a wealthy businessman and his wife posing in their home.

Symbols

The beautiful, expensive fabrics and furnishings in the room reflect the couple's fortune. The oranges on the windowsill also show their wealth. Only the very rich could afford to have fruit shipped from warmer parts of the world.

Van Eyck painted *The Arnolfini Portrait* (1434) on an oak panel.

But what do the other objects show? Oranges were also a symbol of fertility, or the ability to have children. In the front is a dog, a popular symbol of faithfulness at the time. The shoes taken off symbolize that their home is a sacred (holy) place, not to be dirtied by the outside world. What message do you think van Eyck was trying to communicate about this marriage?

Portraits of power

There is a long tradition of portraits of leaders. This statue showing ancient Roman leader Marcus Aurelius uses symbols Romans would have known. The military dress shows he was a military hero. His beard shows he was thoughtful and wise. When the statue was first made, an enemy soldier lay under the horse's foot. Marcus Aurelius's raised right hand means he will spare the soldier's life, showing his kind and fair nature.

If you lived in ancient Rome, how would this statue make you feel about your leader?

This statue of Marcus Aurelius (176 CE) is twice as big as life-sized.

A divided portrait

The self-portrait allows artists to explore their own **identity**. In the self-portrait *The Two Fridas* (1939), Mexican artist Frida Kahlo shows two versions of herself. On the left sits a version dressed in traditional Mexican clothing. On the right sits a version dressed in contemporary, European-style clothing. The hearts of both figures are visible and connected by arteries (tubes that carry blood).

Why the split?

Kahlo had lived through the **context** of the Mexican Revolution (1910–20). Until the revolution, women had few rights or opportunities. Perhaps she felt part of her was a traditional Mexican woman, while part of her was a modern, independent artist.

The stormy skies in *The Two Fridas* (1939) represent Kahlo's troubles. She had just divorced her husband, artist Diego Rivera.

The modern Kahlo supports the hand of the traditional Kahlo. Her heart and arteries are strong and uncut. Which side of her identity do you think Kahlo hoped would win out?

Perform your own portrait

Frida Kahlo showed how she had two different identities. Now explore your own different identities.

Steps to follow:

1. Do you ever feel there are "two" versions of yourself—maybe the version of yourself at home and the version at school? Decide which two versions of yourself you want to explore.

2. Choose clothing that expresses each identity.

3. Find a song that fits each identity.

4. Wear the costume and perform to the song that express your first identity.

If you love ballet, choose a piece of classical music and show some dance positions.

5. Then perform your second identity. If you love soccer, pretend you are in the middle of a game. Choose a song that pumps you up and show some dribbling skills.

After you finish performing, ask your friends or family which version is most like you. Can they think of another side that you didn't show?

Performing can teach you about your identity.

Religious Art

Throughout the centuries, people have used art to honor the god or gods of their religion. Religions around the world use art to inspire believers.

Buddhism

To study religious art, you must understand the **context** of the religion. Buddhism began in Asia. Buddhists honor a man named Siddhartha Gautama, also known as the Buddha. They believe he found **enlightenment**, or a way of living that escapes suffering.

Buddhist writings call for certain symbols when showing the Buddha. For example, a bump on the head symbolizes enlightenment. The pose of sitting with his legs crossed and the soles of his feet visible represents deep thought.

The *Tian Tan Buddha*, also known as the *Big Buddha*, in Hong Kong is one of the world's largest, standing at 34 meters (112 feet).

In terms of **formal elements**, Buddhist writings call for perfect **proportions** (the way parts relate to the whole). This creates a sense of balance. This sculpture helps Buddhists feel peace and balance as they worship.

Hinduism

Hinduism is another ancient Asian religion. Hindus believe that people struggle to break free from a cycle of birth and death.

Worshiping different gods is central to Hindus. One of the most important gods is Shiva, the god of destruction. Destruction is part of life's cycle of birth and death.

Shiva is called "the Lord of Dance."

Shiva's dance

In some sculptures of Shiva, the circular shape symbolizes life's cycles of birth and death. The flames represent destruction. Snakes around Shiva's neck show his power over life and death—he does not fear deadly snakebites. A third eye symbolizes his wisdom.

The sculpture's wild hair and flowing lines suggest movement and action. How is this different from the formal elements of the Buddha?

Christianity

Christians believe that God's son, Jesus Christ, suffered and died for people's sins. Most Christians believe that God, Jesus Christ, and the Holy Spirit are all part of one God.

Raphael and the Renaissance

Christian art hit a high point in Italy during a period called the **Renaissance**, from about 1400 to 1600. Italian Renaissance artists used rich color and a graceful sense of movement, as seen in Raphael's *Sistine Madonna* from about 1513. This painting shows the Virgin Mary (or Madonna), Jesus' human mother, seeming to float from heaven with the baby Jesus. Saints (holy people) and angels surround them.

Raphael's *Sistine Madonna* (c. 1513) is a great Renaissance painting.

What is going on?

Previous works of art like this were peaceful and comforting. In contrast, Raphael's Madonna and Child look at the viewer with looks of horror. But why?

One writer believes a crucifix was placed across from the painting in its original church location. A crucifix is a work of art that shows Jesus dying on a cross. The Madonna and Child perhaps look with horror at this symbol of the suffering that awaits Jesus.

How do you feel when you look at this work? Why?

African religious art

When viewed in a museum or photograph, African religious art cannot be fully **interpreted**. This is because these objects, such as this carved mask, were part of a larger ceremony. A person would wear the mask along with a costume, dancing as music played. While the mask is beautiful on its own, you must see the whole ceremony to truly appreciate it as a work of religious art.

This African tribal mask is from Zimbabwe.

Art of Everyday Life

There is a long tradition of art that records the events of everyday life. These show us an artist's representation of what life was like in different times and places.

Woman at work

Dutch painter Johannes Vermeer often focused on the everyday activities of women. In *The Lacemaker*, from about 1669–70, he shows a young woman sewing.

Formal elements draw the viewer's attention to the young woman and her work. The front area of the painting is blurred. This forces the eye to move up to the area in focus, showing the woman and her sewing. The brightness of the woman's yellow dress and the light falling on her face further attract the viewer's eye to her.

The Lacemaker (c. 1669–70) shows Vermeer's beautiful use of light.

A symbol of virtue

At the time, embroidery work was linked with the Virgin Mary, a symbol of virtue (purity) in the Bible. Hard work was also seen as virtuous. The book on the table is probably a Bible. Vermeer wanted the viewer to see this woman and her work as symbols of virtue.

A tiny painting

The Lacemaker is tiny, at 9.4 by 8.3 inches (24 by 21 centimeters). What effect would this have on the viewer?

Photos of everyday life

In her series *Family Pictures and Stories*, from 1974–84, African American photographer Carrie Mae Weems took photographs of family members doing everyday things. When she displayed her photos in a gallery, voice recordings played alongside the photos. In the recordings, Weems commented on her family and its history. Weems said that examining moments from everyday life taught her about her own **identity** and that of her family.

Carrie Mae Weems created the *Family Pictures and Stories* series from 1978 to 1984.

Create your own "family pictures and stories"

Steps to follow:

1. Gather some favorite photos of family or friends.

2. Organize the pictures by theme—for example, group pictures of certain relatives, or from trips that you have taken.

3. Create a poster photo display for these groups of pictures.

4. When Carrie Mae Weems displayed her photographs, she had her recorded voice play in the background. Write down some thoughts and memories you have about each group of pictures. Write about what these moments from everyday life show you about your own family. Also write about how your family has shaped your identity.

5. Invite family members to come see your photo display. Instead of playing a recording, you will read your prepared thoughts out loud as your family looks at the pictures.

What did your family think of your display and reading? Did they have different thoughts or memories to add?

Family memories can take on new meaning when you share them.

Soup cans

Art that explores everyday life can also look at a **culture**. In 1962 U.S. artist Andy Warhol created 32 paintings of Campbell's soup cans. He lined the paintings up on the wall like soup cans on a grocery store shelf.

This focus on everyday images was at the heart of his **Pop Art** style. So was Warhol's use of **silk-screening**. This printing technique creates works that look like something bought at the store, rather than paintings made by hand.

Consumer goods

The historical **context** was that in the 1950s people in the United States were becoming more wealthy. People became really interested in the idea of buying things.

Warhol's simple works were treated like expensive objects to be admired on the walls of galleries and museums. Warhol perhaps wanted to show how much people spent admiring things they could buy, like these soup cans.

Warhol's *Campbell's Soup Cans* (1962) challenged what people expected art to be.

Pure Form

Some artists explore the basic **formal elements** of art without any **subject matter** (recognizable images). This is called **abstract** art.

Abstract Expressionism

In the early 1940s, U.S. artist Jackson Pollock helped to developed a painting style known as **Abstract Expressionism**. Pollock placed huge canvases on the ground. He used everyday tools like sticks and knives to drip and pour paint directly from a can onto the canvas.

In works like *Painting A* (1960), there is no clear subject matter. Rather, the painting is all about the formal elements—color, texture, line, and movement. The viewer must focus on the form and on the emotions that Pollock expressed while painting.

What emotions do you think Pollock expressed in *Painting A* (1950)?

Is it "art"?

At the time, some people admired Pollock's work. Others did not and felt his work wasn't "art." Do you think art can be powerful even if it doesn't have subject matter?

Open yourself up

Art can be fun, but it can also be challenging. Try to learn all you can about a work of art before you make any judgments. In the process, you will learn about different **cultures**, people, ideas—and even yourself.

Abstract sculpture

Abstract sculptors also explore pure form. In 2007 Indian-born British artist Anish Kapoor created *C-Curve*, an enormous curve made of polished steel. At first it seems to be simply about form—shape and material. However, the curve shows people's reflections. In this way, the appearance of the work changes all the time. It also makes the viewer think about the experience of looking at art.

Kapoor's *C-Curve* (2007) is seen here during an arts' festival in England.

Timeline

30,000 BCE	Artists create the earliest cave paintings.
c. 176 CE	An ancient Roman artist completes a statue of Marcus Aurelius on a horse.
400s	An ancient artist creates an important **stela** in Tikal (present-day Guatemala).
400s	An artist creates an image of Shiva in Tamil Nadu, India.
1434	Jan van Eyck paints *The Arnolfini Portrait* in Bruges (present-day Belgium).
c. 1513	Italian artist Raphael paints the *Sistine Madonna*.
1638-39	Italian artist Artemisia Gentileschi paints a self-portrait called *Self-Portrait as the Allegory of Painting*.
c. 1669—70	Dutch artist Johannes Vermeer paints *The Lacemaker*.
1805	French painter Jacques-Louis David begins work on *The Coronation of Napoleon*.
1821	English artist John Constable paints *The Hay Wain*.
1832	Japanese artist Katsushika Hokusai creates the print *The Great Wave at Kanagawa*.
1885	French artist Claude Monet paints *The Poppy Field near Giverny*.
1937	Spanish artist Pablo Picasso paints *Guernica*.
1939	Mexican artist Frida Kahlo paints *The Two Fridas*.
1950	U.S. artist Jackson Pollock paints *Painting A*.

1962	U.S. artist Andy Warhol creates *Campbell's Soup Cans*.
1978	U.S. artist Carrie Mae Weems begins her *Family Pictures and Stories* series of photographs.
1989	Tribal mask from Zimbabwe is used in ceremony.
1993	*Tian Tan (Big Buddha)* is completed.
2000	Brazilian **photojournalist** Sebastião Salgado publishes a series of photographs called *Migrations.*
2007	Indian-born British artist Anish Kapoor creates the **abstract** sculpture *S-Curve.*

Glossary

abstract lacking clear subject matter

Abstract Expressionism artistic style that uses large canvases, poured and dripped paint, and expressive movement

composition overall arrangement of the parts of a work of art

context background information of the where, when, and how of something

coronation crowning of someone and giving him or her a high office

Cubism artistic style that breaks down objects into nearly abstract geometric shapes and using a flat sense of space

culture set of daily practices, ideas, and interests followed by a group of people in a particular time and place

enlightenment in Buddhism, set of moral and spiritual practices that help one escape the suffering of the world

formal element purely visual feature such as line, color, form, composition, space, and texture in a work of art

identity who a person is and what makes the person that way

Impressionism artistic style that uses quick brushstrokes and sketchy details and usually seeks to achieve the effects of experiencing nature directly

Industrial Revolution period of history in Europe and North America from about 1760 to 1850, when machines and factories increased in number and changed the way many people lived

interpret give meaning to

landscape picture that shows an open view of nature

migration movement of large numbers of people

monument large work of art, often stone or metal, that is put in a public place to remember a person or event

photojournalist person who takes pictures that record events in history

Pop Art artistic style that uses everyday images and printing styles that make paintings look like objects bought in a store rather than artwork made by hand

proportion way different parts relate to the whole

Renaissance period in Europe from about 1400 to 1600 when many great works of art were created and ideas were explored

silk screen printing process that pushes paint or ink through a screen made of silk onto canvas or paper

stela stone slab with carvings

subject matter in art, content—for example, images of people or places

woodblock printing printing technique in which an artist carves wooden blocks, dips them in ink, and prints them onto paper

Find Out More

Books

d'Harcourt, Claire. *Masterpieces Up Close: Western Painting from the 14th to 20th Centuries*. San Francisco: Chronicle, 2006.

Dickins, Rosie. *The Usbourne Art Treasury*. Tulsa, Okla.: EDC, 2007.

Renshaw, Amanda, and Gilda Williams Ruggi. *The Art Book for Children*. New York: Phaidon, 2005.

Websites

National Gallery of Art
www.nga.gov/kids
Learn about art and create your own at this website just for kids.

Museum of Modern Art
http://www.moma.org/interactives/destination/
Explore modern art at this interactive website.

Places to visit

You can see a range of art at the following museums, or at your local museums.

National Gallery of Art
4th and Constitution Ave. NW
Washington, DC 20565
www.nga.gov

Metropolitan Museum of Art
1000 Fifth Ave.
New York, NY 10028-0198
www.metmuseum.org

The Art Institute of Chicago
111 S. Michigan Ave.
Chicago, IL
60603-6404
www.artic.edu

Index